CORNWALL
NARROW GAUGE
including the Camborne & Redruth Tramway

Maurice Dart

Series editor Vic Mitchell

MP Middleton Press

*Cover pictures. Upper: Pentewan Railway 0-6-2ST **Canopus** waits on the trestle alongside the harbour at Pentewan in 1912. The locomotive was built by Manning Wardle in 1901, works no.1547. (M.Dart coll.)*

*Lower: This is a scene at New Mills, which is the western terminus of the Launceston Steam Railway. A train headed by 0-4-0ST **Lilian** waits to return to Launceston on 10th May 1998. The locomotive was built by the Hunslet Engine Co in 1883 and was works no.317. It formerly worked at Penrhyn Quarry, North Wales. (Mrs K.Bowman)*

Back: Camborne & Redruth Tramway car no. 4 waits near Barncoose Loop in this fine postcard view. (R.J.Harley coll.)

Published May 2005

ISBN 1 904474 56 X

© Middleton Press, 2005

Design David Pede

Published by
> *Middleton Press*
> *Easebourne Lane*
> *Midhurst, West Sussex*
> *GU29 9AZ*

Tel: 01730 813169
Fax: 01730 812601
Email: info@middletonpress.co.uk
www.middletonpress.co.uk

Printed & bound by Biddles Ltd, Kings Lynn

15.   Mineral tram no.2 has descended Pool Hill on its way from East Pool mine to Tolvaddon stamps in the earlier period of the lines existence. (M.Dart coll.)

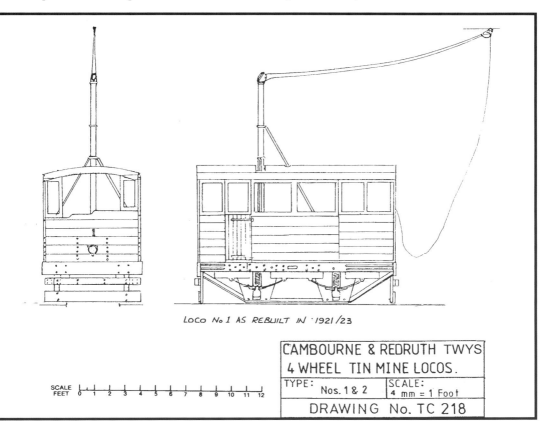

LOCO No 1 AS REBUILT IN ·1921/23

CAMBOURNE & REDRUTH TWYS		
4 WHEEL TIN MINE LOCOS.		
TYPE: Nos. 1 & 2		SCALE: 4 mm = 1 Foot
DRAWING No. TC 218		

SCALE FEET 0 1 2 3 4 5 6 7 8 9 10 11 12

16.   In this interesting scene from the early 1900s, car no.4 is closely followed by mineral tram no.1 with a train at Trevenson. The lady with the white headdress and apron was a *Bal-Maiden,* a lady mineworker. (Pamlin Prints/M.Dart coll.)

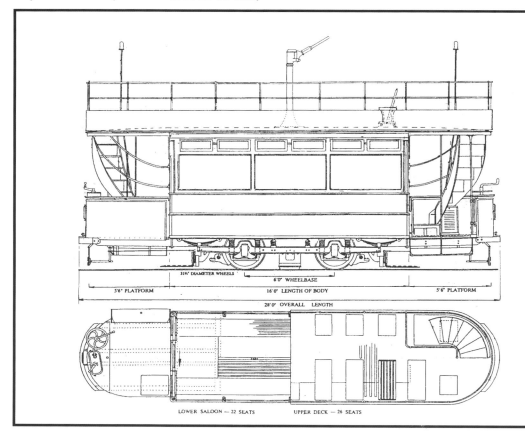

31¼" DIAMETER WHEELS   6'0" WHEELBASE

5'6" PLATFORM   16'0" LENGTH OF BODY   5'6" PLATFORM

28'0" OVERALL LENGTH

LOWER SALOON — 22 SEATS   UPPER DECK — 26 SEATS

17.   As we look east rebuilt mineral trams no.2 and no.1 are passing with trains at Trevenson loop in the early 1930s. (Cornwall Studies Library)

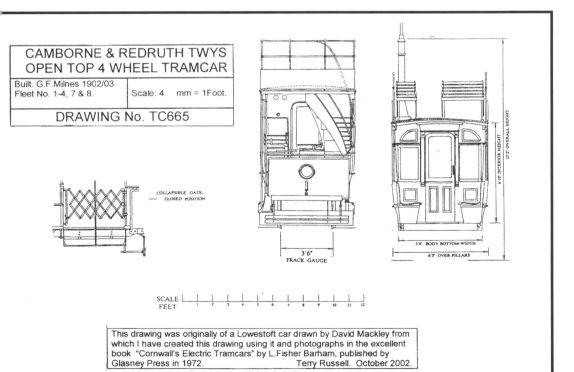

CAMBORNE & REDRUTH TWYS
OPEN TOP 4 WHEEL TRAMCAR

Built. G.F.Milnes 1902/03
Fleet No. 1-4, 7 & 8.   Scale: 4   mm = 1Foot.

DRAWING No. TC665

COLLAPSIBLE GATE
— CLOSED POSITION

6'10" INTERIOR HEIGHT

13'7" OVERALL HEIGHT

3'6"
TRACK GAUGE

5'6" BODY BOTTOM WIDTH

6'3" OVER PILLARS

SCALE
FEET   1   2   3   4   5   6   7   8   9   10   11   12

This drawing was originally of a Lowestoft car drawn by David Mackley from which I have created this drawing using it and photographs in the excellent book "Cornwall's Electric Tramcars" by L.Fisher Barham, published by Glasney Press in 1972.   Terry Russell. October 2002.

AVAILABLE FROM :—TERRY RUSSELL, "CHACESIDE", ST.LEONARDS PARK, HORSHAM, W.SUSSEX. RH13 6EG.
SEND 3 FIRST CLASS STAMPS FOR COMPLETE LIST OF PUBLIC TRANSPORT DRAWINGS.

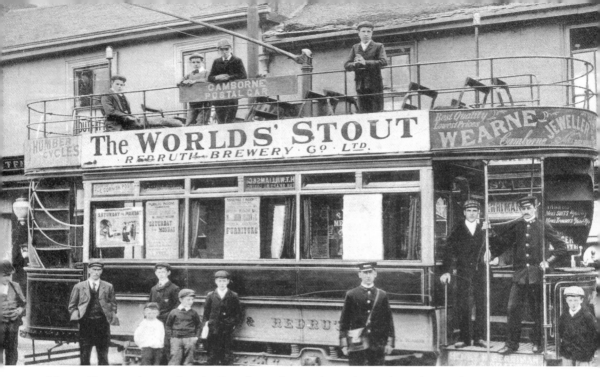

18.   Tram no.1, carrying the Postal car sign, waits to depart from the Pendarves Street stop at Camborne in 1904. Even the step carries an advertisement. (M.Dart coll.)

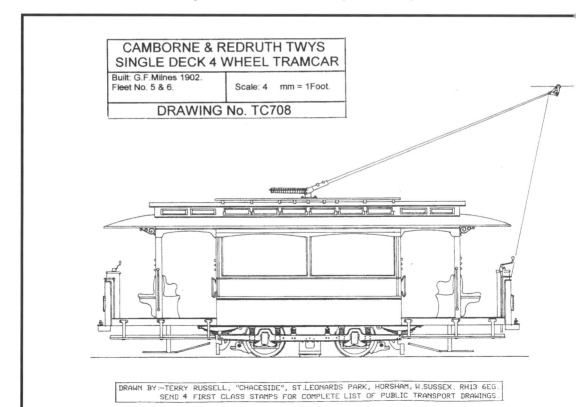

CAMBORNE & REDRUTH TWYS
SINGLE DECK 4 WHEEL TRAMCAR

Built: G.F.Milnes 1902.
Fleet No. 5 & 6.

Scale: 4   mm = 1Foot.

DRAWING No. TC708

DRAWN BY:-TERRY RUSSELL, "CHACESIDE", ST.LEONARDS PARK, HORSHAM, W.SUSSEX. RH13 6EG.
SEND 4 FIRST CLASS STAMPS FOR COMPLETE LIST OF PUBLIC TRANSPORT DRAWINGS.

19.	Cars 5 and 6 had an exceptionally short saloon. Each side of it can be seen the lifeguards which would scoop up any errant pedestrians. (R.J.Harley coll.)

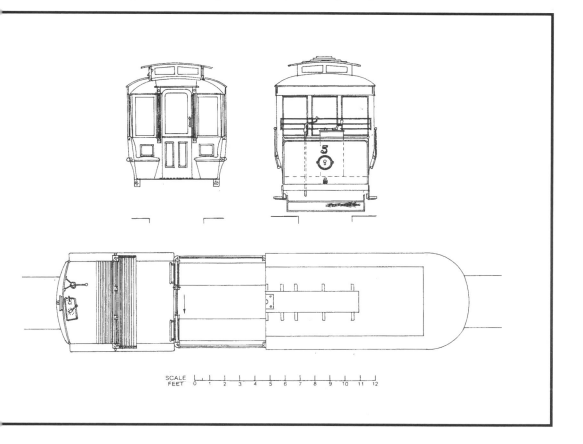

SCALE
FEET	0 1 2 3 4 5 6 7 8 9 10 11 12

CARBIS BRICK WORKS TRAMWAY, BUGLE

A china clay works opened at Carbis in 1858 and a brick works followed in 1883. A 2ft gauge tramway was laid to bring clay 350yd to the brick works. The line crossed a lane on the level and ran in a deep cutting that was spanned by two bridges that carried rough tracks. The empty wagon was pushed up manually, and when loaded ran back by gravity with the boys riding on it. The line closed in 1942.

IV.   This diagrammatic map shows details of the line in May 1957. (M.Dart/ S.Parkinson)

V.   The tramway is shown on this map from 1907. It runs southwest from near the terminus of the GWRs Carbis Wharf branch.

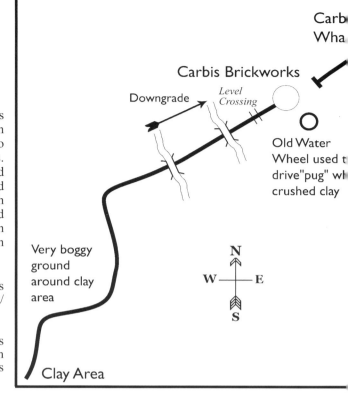

Carbi
Wha

Carbis Brickworks

Downgrade   Level Crossing

Old Water
Wheel used t
drive"pug" wh
crushed clay

Very boggy ground around clay area

Clay Area

N
W — E
S

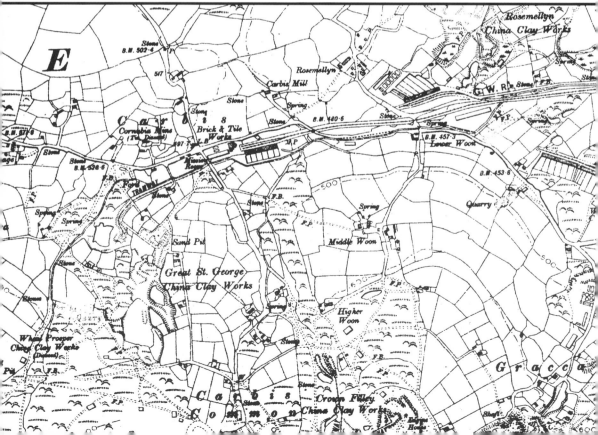

20.   This is how to turn a tramway into a river! In the last decade, during flood prevention work, a river was partly diverted along the trackbed. We look west and see rails that remained, partly submerged, in the cutting between the two bridges on 28th February 2004. (M.Dart)

21.   Looking west, on 18th March 2004, we view the first of the substantially constructed bridges over the line. (M.Dart)

CHARLESTOWN NO.1 CHINA CLAY KILN, ST.AUSTELL

A coal fired pan kiln was built near to the harbour in 1908. Clay was tipped through hatches in the floor of the linhay into wagons that ran on a line in a tunnel. It ended above a grating through which the clay was tipped to a storage area known as a Surge Bin that was hewn out of rock. A second line ran in tunnels from the Surge Bin to chutes above the harbour. Both lines were laid to a gauge of 2ft 4in. The kiln ceased drying clay in the 1960s. The upper entrance has been sealed but wagons remain inside both tunnels.

22.   The kiln now forms part of the Shipwreck Centre. Members of the Branch Line Society examined the tunnel entrance on 30th May 1992 during a visit. Rails remained inside the tunnel. (M.Dart)

23.   During the visit by the BLS, permission was obtained for members to proceed along the tunnel, for which some gates were unlocked. We look towards gates at the entrance to the Surge Bin where the tunnel forked. Both sections were unlit, but wagons could be discerned on one of the lines. (M.Dart)

DELABOLE SLATE QUARRY

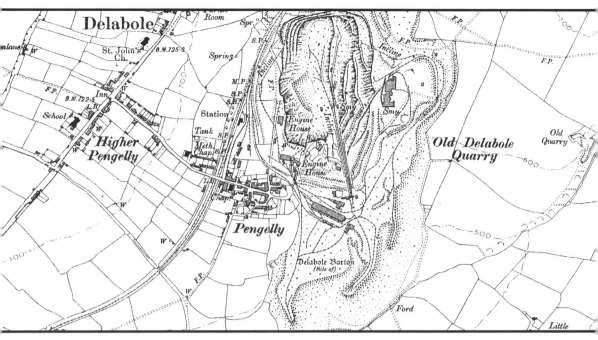

VI.   The narrow gauge lines in the quarry are shown on this map from 1907, together with the siding from the LSWR's North Cornwall line.

24.   Slate has been quarried here since the sixteenth century and was worked for many years by the Old Delabole Slate Co Ltd. From 1834 haulage up the inclines was by a stationary steam engine and tramroads were laid from 1841. This pre-1922 view at the head of the incline shows horse traction in use on 1ft 11in gauge track. (J.Vaughan coll.)

25.   Steam locomotives were introduced in 1879 and this is an 0-4-0ST built by the Hunslet Engine Co in that year, works no.219. It is named *E.Jago* and is on the top of the quarry on the south side. It was scrapped during 1930. (R.I.C.Photographic Collection. Ref MI del 013)

26.   The quarry remains in production and is operated by Delabole Slate (1977) Ltd. The centrepiece of the visitor centre is preserved 4wDM no.2, which is seen on 1st August 2001. It was built by Motor Rail in 1925 and is works no.3739. (M.Dart)

Further views appear in *Branch Line to Padstow.*

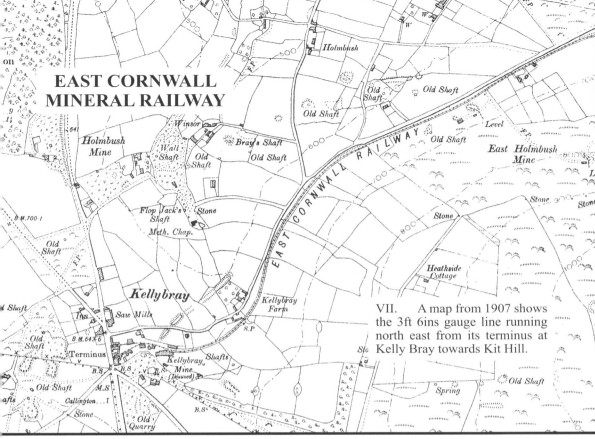

EAST CORNWALL MINERAL RAILWAY

VII. A map from 1907 shows the 3ft 6ins gauge line running north east from its terminus at Kelly Bray towards Kit Hill.

The Callington & Calstock Railway was authorised on 9th August 1869 to build a 7½ mile line from Kelly Bray to west of Calstock, from where it descended by an incline to a quay on the River Tamar. It changed its name to the East Cornwall Mineral Railway and opened on 7th May 1872. Short branches served several mines and quarries. The line carried copper, tin and arsenic ore from the mines to the quay for shipment, and conveyed coal, timber and other supplies back to the mines. On 25th August 1883 an act authorised the Plymouth, Devonport & South Western Junction Railway to purchase the line and extend it to Beer (later Bere) Alston. The PDSWJR took the ECMR over on 1st June 1891, but did not complete the actual purchase until 4th January 1894. The new line opened on 2nd March 1908 when the original one was closed. As rebuilding progressed, the line was dual gauge and was only closed for two days over the whole period. The incline to Calstock Quay was abandoned after construction of a wagon hoist from the viaduct to the quay.

27. An overline bridge at the top of the incline from the quay together with the engine house, topped by a water tank, are viewed on 31st March 1990 during a visit by the Cornwall Railway Society. A 14hp stationary engine powered the cable-worked incline. Lines passed each side of the building. (M.Dart)

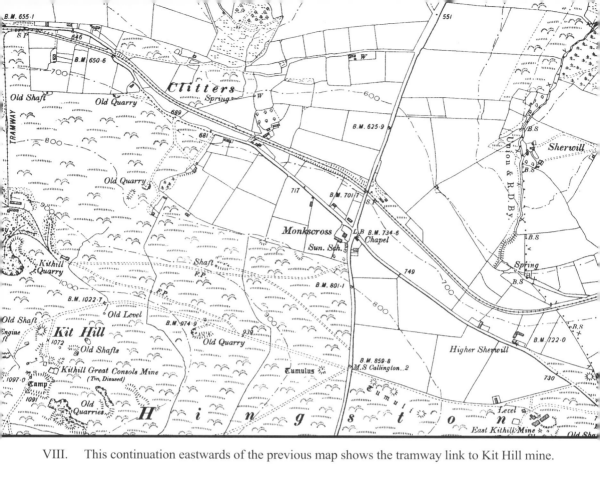

VIII.   This continuation eastwards of the previous map shows the tramway link to Kit Hill mine.

28.   The locomotive shed was at the top of the incline. One of the line's pair of 0-4-0STs, no.1, in original condition, stands outside. It was works no.1660 built by Neilson & Co in 1871 and is believed to have been scrapped on site in 1909. (M.Dart coll.)

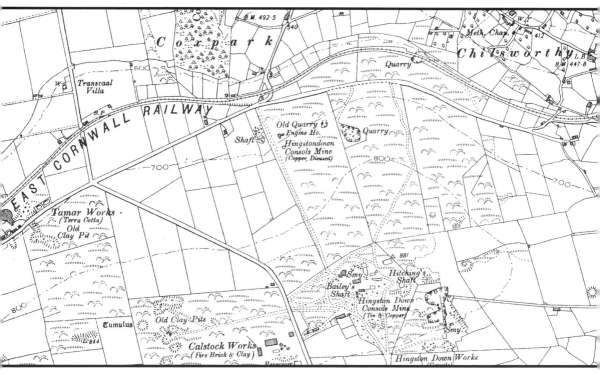

IX.   This shows the line as it headed east across Hingston Down to Chilsworthy.

29.   We are looking almost north up the River Tamar in this 1908 view of the ECMR incline and quay at Calstock. The newly completed viaduct with the wagon hoist is well depicted, as a pleasure paddle steamer heads up the river towards Morwellham and Weir Head. (M.Dart coll.)

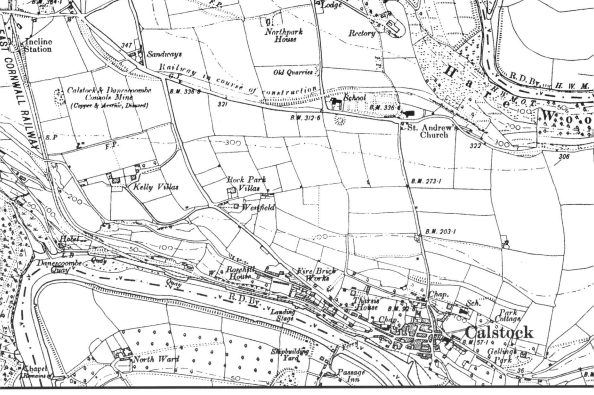

X.   From Chilsworthy the line headed south. This map shows the line as it descended a rope worked incline to Calstock Quay.

30.   The quay at Calstock is seen in ECMR days, with wagons visible to the left. The trestle tower in the background is part of the equipment being used in the construction of the viaduct; that dates the scene as 1905. (M.Dart coll.)

GEEVOR MINE, PENDEEN

This tin mine was a combination of several smaller mines, which included South Geevor and North Levant, on the Atlantic coast west of Pendeen. Mining had started here before 1806 and ceased by October 1991. Some of the equipment, including locomotives, was removed and sold. However a few locomotives remain in deep workings that are flooded. By August 1993 it had been taken over by Cornwall County Council to be developed as a heritage site. An extensive system of 1ft 6in gauge lines existed, mostly underground at different levels. Parts of the site have been opened to the public as Geevor Tin Mines Museum.

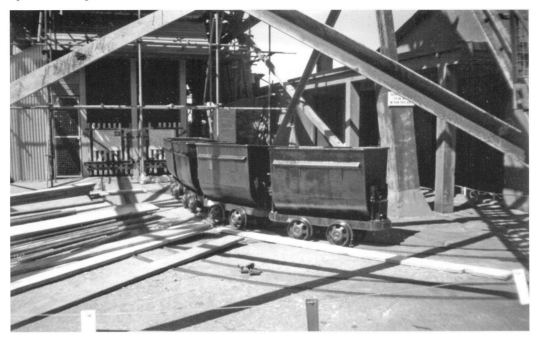

31.   During a visit on 27th April 1998 some renovated skip wagons were recorded standing by the entrance to the main shaft. (M.Dart)

32.   During the same visit, permission was obtained to enter the engineering shop, which was not normally open to the public. At the rear were two rows of 4w battery electric locomotives which in some places, were double stacked. This view includes no.70 with at least nine others. (M.Dart)

33.   A further visit was arranged for some members of the Branch Line Society on 4th June 1998. Three 4wBE locomotives were recorded inside the locked charging shed by putting the camera through a gap in the boarded up door. They were nos.74 and 91 with one occupant unidentified. (M.Dart)

34.   During the second visit, 4wBE no.49 was standing outside the empty locomotive shop, which adjoined the first floor of the engineering shop. (M.Dart)

HENDRA CHINA STONE QUARRY, NANPEAN

35.   This quarry had been worked since around the 1860s and a system of 2ft 3in gauge lines had been laid. The layout changed as different working areas opened. Here we look west on the floor of the quarry in the 1920s. (Imerys Minerals)

36.   Stone was brought to the surface by rail, using cable worked inclines. During a visit by members of Plymouth Railway Circle on 22nd April 1967, we look down on this panorama of the quarry from the top of one of the inclines. The line leading off towards the top left of the picture tunnelled through the rock and entered an adjacent quarry. (M.Dart)

HENDRA LIGHT RAILWAY,
NANPEAN

37.   This 2ft gauge line ran for three quarters of a mile from below the linhay of Hendra china clay kiln. It ran south to a storage shed by a loading wharf alongside the GWR siding at Quarry Close, near Drinnick Mill. The store had a capacity of 4000 tons. The line operated from 1919 to around 1939, and used a 20hp 4w petrol locomotive which was built by Motor Rail in 1918, works no.862. We see the locomotive bringing a loaded train from the kiln in around 1921. (Imerys Minerals)

38.   Between Hendra and Quarry Close the line ran alongside the road from Nanpean to St.Dennis and crossed it on the level. We look northwest in 1921 and see the train after it has left Hendra. The wagons had a capacity of 2.5tons. Sand tips from Hendra clay pit are in the background. (Imerys Minerals)

MELBUR CHINA CLAY PIT, ST.STEPHEN

39.   At china clay pits, the soil (overburden) that covered the clay beds had to be removed as the area occupied by the pit expanded. Narrow gauge tramways were laid at many pits to move the material to a tip. Some tips were quite a distance away on the opposite side of the pit. The wagons were propelled manually, by horses, or later, in a few locations, by a small diesel locomotive. This interesting scene from the early 1920s shows the burden plat at Melbur pit with a manually worked three line tramway. An early excavator is in use for burden removal. Redundant lines that led around the pit have been partly removed. Conical sky tips of sand from four adjacent pits are visible on the skyline. The tramway incline on the right tip has a bridge over a road. (Imerys Minerals)

44.　　On the same date, another 4wD is propelling wagons towards the crushers from the east for loading. (R.Winnen)

45.　　This panorama looks east from the crushers towards Newlyn in June 1972. A loaded train is departing to Newlyn as empties are being propelled back to be re-loaded. A third diesel locomotive can be seen in the distance. (R.Winnen)

46.	On the same date, a locomotive with a loaded train is approaching the curve that led to the quay at Newlyn. (R.Winnen)

47.	This scene looks south along the quay on a wet day in the early 1980s. Rails still remain and the conveyor belt system that replaced the railway is on the left. (R.Winnen)

PENTEWAN DOCK & CONCRETE COMPANY

This was originally called Pentewan Dock Ltd, and in 1965 it became known as Pentewan Sands Ltd. Sand extraction commenced in 1939 and ceased in 1966. The line carried sand from dunes to classifiers situated west of the harbour entrance. Concrete blocks were also produced at the site. Lines that ran along the quay were used when shunting was taking place. The gauge of 2ft 6in was identical to that used by the Pentewan Railway and some of the lines on the quay were on the earlier lines formation.

48. When visited during evenings or at weekends the locomotives were inside one of two sheds. The newer structure was constructed of concrete blocks and could accommodate two engines. It was in the fork of the junction of the lines to the dunes and to the harbour mouth. The shed was not at all photogenic and the occupants could be glimpsed through holes in a shuttered window. We see an older engine and wagon shed on 7th September 1988 that was constructed of brick and had been re-roofed and refurbished. A siding

off the line that extended south towards the beach provided access to it. (P.G.Barnes)

49. The company possessed three locomotives and all worked here and at the company's other works at Gwithian, near Hayle. The works at Gwithian closed in October 1958 and all of the engines went to Pentewan. Two were scrapped but one has survived. It is seen on 23rd July 1987 at Wheal Martyn China Clay Museum. It was built in 1946 by Ruston & Hornsby,works no.244558. (M.Dart)

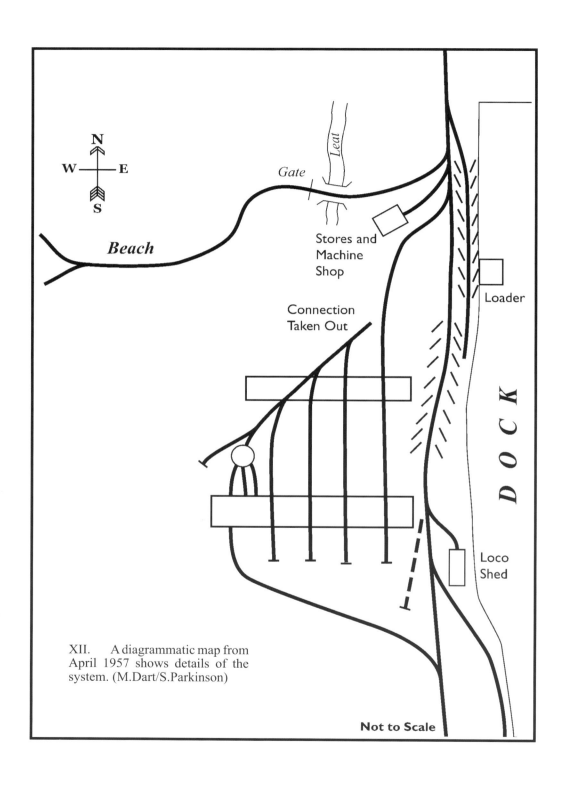

N

W — E

S

Leat

Gate

Beach

Stores and
Machine
Shop

Loader

Connection
Taken Out

D O C K

Loco
Shed

XII.   A diagrammatic map from
April 1957 shows details of the
system. (M.Dart/S.Parkinson)

Not to Scale

PENTEWAN RAILWAY

This line was constructed as a 4ft gauge horse-worked line in 1829, without parliamentary powers. It ran for three and a half miles and linked St.Austell with Pentewan, where there was a harbour. The valley that it ran through had possessed copper and tin mines, and also stone quarries. But the main object was to provide transport to the harbour from numerous china clay works that were developing in the area surrounding St.Austell. The undertaking was officially recognised by Acts dated 1862 and 1867 and was incorporated as the Pentewan Railway & Harbour Co Ltd on 20th February 1873. Following an Act dated 7th August 1874 the line was rebuilt to a gauge of 2ft 6in and steam traction was authorised. Two branch lines were proposed to access the china clay works in the Gover and the Trenance valleys north of St.Austell. Neither of these materialised but the GWR later built the Lansalson branch up the Trenance valley. Proposed extensions to the main line station in St.Austell and to Mevagissey were not constructed. Reservoirs were constructed at Pentewan to flush out accumulations of clay, sand and other minerals from the harbour, but despite this measure the harbour eventually became completely silted up and unusable. This led to the demise of the line, with complete closure taking place on 4th March 1918. This is simply an outline of the line's complex existence.

50.　　We look north from the terminus of the railway at West Hill, St.Austell in 1910. A wagon loaded with clay, drawn by three horses, has arrived in the yard for unloading, either into rail wagons or a clay store at the site. There are small stone blocks at the end of the lines instead of buffers. This site now forms the frontage of the Co-operative Group store. (Imerys Minerals)

XIII. This map from 1907 shows the line as it headed south from St.Austell, past New Mills and London Apprentice.

XIV.   Almost continuous with the previous
map, this shows the line as it passed Kings
Wood and entered Pentewan.

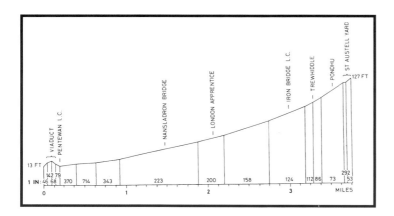

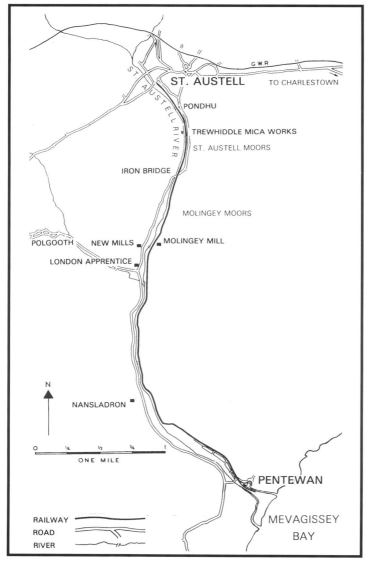

XV.　This map shows the complete route of the line as built. (M.J.Messenger/ Twelve Heads Press)

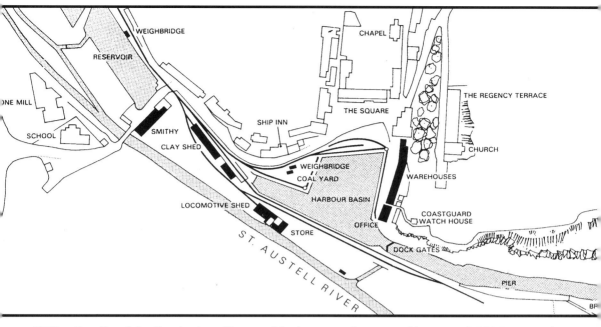

XVI.   Details of the line in the village and harbour are shown on this map. (M.J.Messenger/
Twelve Heads Press)

51.   This   view   of
0-6-2ST *Canopus* on 8th
July 1915 looks north up
the valley. The engine is
hauling wagons carrying
people from St.Austell on a
Sunday School treat. A wind
pump, a water tank and the
lower reservoir are in the
left centre of the picture.
The upper reservoir is just
visible by the bottom of the
vanes on the wind pump.
(LGRP/M.Dart coll.)

52.   We are looking east as 0-6-2ST *Pioneer* passes the lower reservoir on 14th August 1912. It is about to enter Pentewan village where it will cross the road on the level. The engine that was built by the Yorkshire Engine Co in 1903, works no.757, has odd front buffers. It later worked at WD Sunbury and at WD Newbury. (K.Smith coll.)

53.   Looking east, soon after 1886, we see 0-6-0 *Trewithen* on the west side of the harbour. The engine was built by Manning Wardle in 1886, works no.994, and was scrapped during 1901 The raised line on which wagons were positioned for unloading into ships can be seen behind the engine. (M.Dart coll.)

54. This is a rare picture of almost new 0-6-0 *Pentewan* with wagons on the raised loading line on the west side of the harbour in 1874. This was another product of Manning Wardle, works no.461 which was built in 1874. Lumps of clay are lying beside the supports of the loading line ramp. This engine was withdrawn in 1886 and was scrapped in 1896. (M.Dart coll.)

55. Again on the west side of the dock almost level with the lock gates, is 0-6-2ST *Canopus*. This engine was a product of Manning Wardle, works no.1547, built in 1901. It later worked at WD West Drayton. The harbourmasters office, which is still extant, is behind the rear of the engine and is seen in 1905. (J.Vaughan coll.)

56. We look north at the harbour around 1900 from in front of the harbourmasters office. Empty wagons, and one loaded with coal, are on the lines on the east side. The elevated loading line can be seen on the west side of the dock. The weigh-bridge building is visible behind the mast and rigging of the nearest ship. (J.Vaughan coll.)

POCHINS TRAMWAY, GOTHERS, ENNISCAVEN, ST.DENNIS

This was one of the most difficult lines on which to obtain factual information. H.D.Pochin purchased china clay works at Higher Gothers and at Wheal Frederick in 1879. He constructed a railway line from the works that ran across the Goss Moor to a loading wharf alongside the Cornwall Minerals Railway line from Drinnick Mill to St.Dennis Junction. Clay dried in the kilns at Gothers was taken by train from the wharf to either Newquay for shipment or to Melangoose Mill on the Retew branch for milling. Coal was taken back to Gothers. The line opened in 1880, although one source quotes 1884. An Act dated 9th September 1884 authorised construction of the line. The transhipment wharf was known as Pochins, Domellick or Melangoose siding. The Act that authorised the line stated that the gauge should be at least 2ft 9in, but some sources have quoted it as being laid to the gauge of 3ft 1in. The engines that were used on the line were all originally 3ft gauge. Steam traction was used from the outset, and four locomotives worked on the line. All were 0-4-0STs with outside cylinders. Earthworks, such as embankments for the line. were built using waste sand from nearby china clay works. The sleepers used were made of wood from old ex Battle of Trafalgar ships and were studded with nails. An agreement dated 7th March 1916 authorised a loop and additional sidings to serve Wheal Frederick. In 1920 a steeply graded branch line was opened from Lower Gothers to Varcoes Mica kiln. The system closed completely during 1933. The first locomotive was *Dinah,* which was built by Hawthorn in 1880 and was scrapped in the early 1930s. The second was *Crookfoot,* which was a product of either Barclay or Andrew Barclay. *Brooke,* the third engine, was Hudswell Clarke, works no.495 of 1898. It and *Crookfoot* were sold for scrap. The last locomotive, *Greenfold,* arrived in 1931 and saw little use. It was works no.1428, built by the Hunslet Engine Co. in 1922. This last engine did not carry its name whilst at Gothers. It remained in the engine shed until it was scrapped in 1953.

57.   This view, dated 12th June 1989, looks south inside the works area. Gothers no.2 kiln is on the right. The locomotive repair shed is to the left of the centre. The shell of the engine shed was behind the camera to the left and was buried in trees and other vegetation. (M.Dart)

58.   Here we have a close up view of the locomotive repair shed on 12th June 1989. The original, very rusty, water tank is still in position and in use. As well as a being a repair shop, the building had been used to stable one spare engine. After the line closed the building continued in use for servicing motor vehicles. (M.Dart)

REDRUTH & CHASEWATER RAILWAY

This was a prime example of an early Victorian mineral line that never carried passengers. Its sole purpose was to carry ores from copper mines in the Gwennap district, south of Redruth and Chasewater, to the harbours at Point and Devoran for shipment. It transported coal and timber back to the mines. It was a private line that was owned and operated by John Taylor & Sons. It was authorised by an Act dated 17th June 1824. The first section from Wheal Buller to Narabo quays east of Devoran opened on 30th January 1826. An extension to Devoran followed on 6th November 1826. This was followed during 1827 by a line from Lanner Hill to Redruth and the section from Devoran to Point Quay. The line was laid to the gauge of 4ft and was horse-worked until locomotives were introduced from 1st December 1854. Between 1847 and 1851 the line was extended west for half a mile from Wheal Buller to East Basset stamps and South Wheal Francis mines. There is a possibility that it was extended even further for a short period. It closed west of Wheal Buller at an unknown date. Substantial earthworks for a branch line from Hale Mills to mines at Wheal Busy in the Poldice valley were built in 1853, but rails were laid for only a short distance on that section. That was the closest that the line came to approaching the second place in its title. With the decline of the mining industry, traffic on the line dwindled away and complete closure took place on 25th September 1915. The line covered nine and a third miles from Redruth to Devoran, with a further mile to Wheal Buller. The route to Wheal Busy and the extension to South Francis would have added a further mile or so.

XX. Gradient profile of the RCR. (M.J.Messenger, Twelve Heads Press)

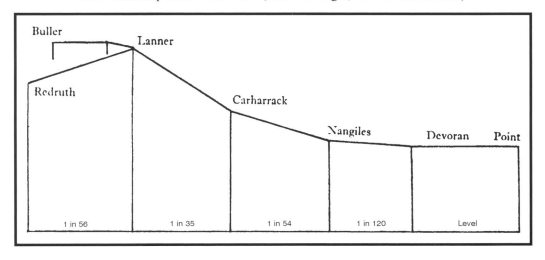

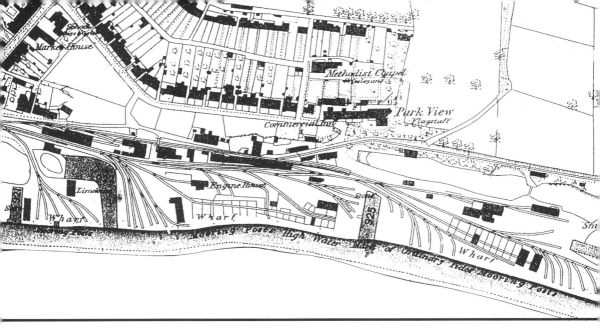

XXI.   This 1st edition at 20ins to one mile map shows the layout of the lines at Devoran together with the line running east to Penpol in about the 1880s.

65.   Eight ore storage hutches (storage bins) remain on Narabo (New) Quay at Devoran. As with all of the storage yards on the line, the rails ran over the top and ore was tipped from the wagons. We see four of the hutches on 26th July 2003, most of which are used to accommodate small boats. (M.Dart)

66.   The replacement locomotive shed has become a private residence but most of the original features have been retained such as the stone arch and rectangular entrance door. The building is seen on 11th April 1995. (M.Dart)

67.   Neilson 0-4-2T *Smelter* is seen standing outside the third engine shed at Devoran in the early 1900s. The engine was built in 1854 as a 0-4-0T and rebuilt with trailing wheels in 1856. The side of the tank has been patched in several places. (M.Dart coll.)

68.   We look southeast to Restronguet creek and view the ruins of the second engine shed on one of the derelict quays at Devoran in the late 1950s. This building, which had latterly seen use as a coal store, had replaced an original timber structure on the quays that had burnt down in 1863. In the left distance some buildings can be seen at Penpol, which was the eastern terminus of the line. (D.Lawrence/H.Davies photos.)

69.   A little farther west in Devoran brings us to the railway workshops that now serve as the village hall and a doctors surgery. This view of the building looks east in the early 1950s. Railway lines ran along each side of the building. (M.Dart coll.)

76.   In this view from the early 1900s, 0-6-0ST *Miner* is heading west, climbing the incline from the level crossing near Crofthandy to Carharrick. Consols Mine dumps are in the background.
(M.Dart coll.)

77.   At the west end of Carharrick village the line crossed the road to the top of Lanner Hill. Shortly after this a footbridge that spanned the line has survived and details are inscribed obn the stone. This is viewed from the west side on 19th August 2003. The trackbed beneath it has been built up somewhat over the years.
(M.Dart)

XXIV. This map is from 1907.

78. At the top of Lanner Hill, the line to Redruth turned off north and ran down a gradient to end a short distance from the site of the later main line station. The site of the terminus has survived together with two lines of granite setts. It is featured in this view which was taken during an exploration by members of Launceston Railway Circle on 3rd July 1999. (M.Dart)

79.   This eastward view shows 0-6-0ST *Miner* with a train of empty wagons passing over a foot crossing between Lanner Hill and Wheal Buller in the early 1900s. (J.Vaughan coll.)

80.   As well as at Devoran, there were storage yards for ore and coal at Crofthandy east of Carharrick (the Great yard), at the west end of Carharrick, Pennance and at Wheal Buller. Parts of these have survived. Rails ran over the tops of them to facilitate emptying ore or coal from wagons. We look into one of the sections of Wheal Buller yard on 17th August 2003. (M.Dart)

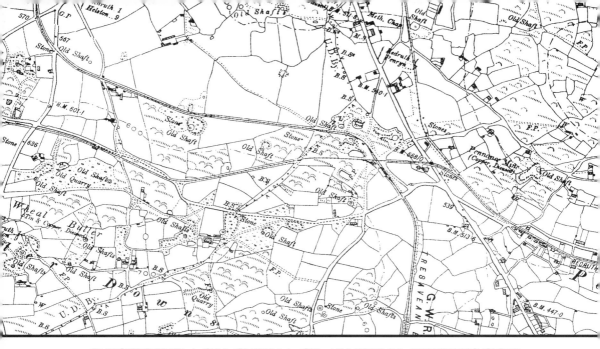

RESTOWRACK CHINA CLAY KILN, TREVISCOE

81.   A 2ft gauge manually worked tramway ran from a loading wharf alongside, and above, the end of Little Treviscoe siding on the branch line from Burngullow to St.Dennis junction. It commenced operating in March 1907 and ceased to be used by August 1969. It passed through a bridge that carried loading equipment for china stone and entered a curved tunnel. This passed under a road near Slip bridge and ended below the linhay of Restowrack or Bowser china clay kiln. Rails could still be found in the tunnel, which we view from the entrance on 16th February 1994. (M.Dart)

92.   Permission was obtained to visit the surface remains at South Crofty on 2nd June 1998. Battery electric locomotives, nos.41, 60 and 47, await disposal in the yard. Two of these were removed during the visit. (M.Dart)

93.   During the visit we were permitted to thoroughly explore all of the surface remains. Here, several ore carrying wagons are gathered, off the track, near the headgear of the main shaft. (M.Dart)

94.   Near the entrance to the main shaft this Crash wagon was awaiting its fate. It presumably carried re-railing equipment. (M.Dart)

2. Pleasure

FRONTIER CITY & RETALLACK ADVENTURE PARK, ST. COLUMB MAJOR

105.　　An American style Wild West theme park was established at this site. It was planned to have a steam worked railway running around the perimeter of the site and one locomotive arrived. A further seven locomotives were due at the site, but that part of the project was not progressed. The 1524mm gauge locomotive, no.1103, that was obtained from Finland, remained on display in an unrestored condition. It is seen on 30th March 1994, during a visit to the rather remote location. (M.Dart)

INNY VALLEY RAILWAY, TRECARRELL MILL, TREBULLETT, LAUNCESTON

Mr J.J.A.Evans owned this private preservation scheme. A circular track of 1ft 10¾in gauge, several hundred yards in length, was laid in a field adjoining the mill buildings, and a workshop was established on the site. Locomotives of 2ft and 550mm gauge were also at the site. Operations commenced in 1968 and ceased in November 1987.

106. Plymouth Railway Circle visited the site on a very wet 12th November 1978. Alongside the rudimentary water tank is 0-4-0ST *Sybil*, built by Bagnalls in 1906, works no.1760. It had previously worked at Dinorwic slate quarries, Llanberis. The locomotive had been towed out from the workshop by 4wDM no.3, a Motor Rail product built in 1950, works no.9546, which is to the rear. After the line closed the saddle tank went to the Launceston Steam Railway and the diesel to Alan Keef Ltd. (M.Dart)

107. After inspecting the locomotive stock, a special train was run around the system. In pouring rain, it is ready to depart for a couple of circuits of the line. The home-made open passenger coach was mainly constructed from sections of redundant church pews. (M.Dart)

LAPPA VALLEY
RAILWAY

This 15 inch gauge line was laid along the track bed of a section of the ex-GWR line from Newquay to Perranporth, which had closed to all traffic on 4th February 1963. The tourist miniature railway opened on 16th June 1974 and runs for one mile from Benny Halt on a rising gradient of 1 in 100 to East Wheal Rose. A leisure area has been formed around the shell of the mine engine house and chimney.

Two miniature railways that operate at East Wheal Rose are a 10¼in gauge line to Newlyn Downs and the 7¼in gauge circular Woodland Railway that runs around the wildlife pond, the woodland, and the Trevithick brick path maze. The two steam locomotives can each haul ten tons, and are capable of pulling a train of five carriages carrying one hundred people up the gradient to East Wheal Rose.

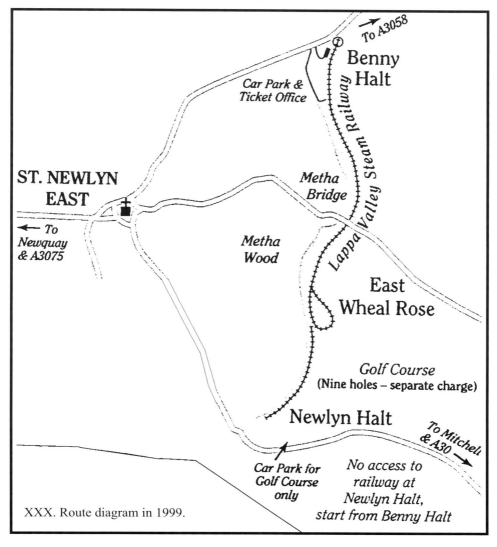

XXX. Route diagram in 1999.

BENNY HALT

108.　　We look north east at the terminus at Benny Halt on 31st May 1992, during a visit by members of the Branch Line Society. 0-6-4T no.1 *Zebedee* waits to depart on an afternoon train to East Wheal Rose. The locomotive was built by Severn-Lamb as an 0-6-2T in 1974 and was converted to an 0-6-4T during 1990. (M.Dart)

109.　　Standing under the canopy at Benny Halt on 20th July 1999 is 4-4wDH *Gladiator*. This was originally a diesel electric named *Lappa Lady* that was built by Minirail around 1960, and was obtained from the Axe & Lyme Valleys Light Railway in July 1976. It was rebuilt in 1980 and again in 1986. (M.Dart)

110. In this scene we see 0-6-0 no.2 *Muffin* inside the two-road engine shed at Benny Halt on 31st May 1992. It was built by Berwyn in 1967 and was rebuilt in 1991. The locomotive had also worked on ALVLR and came to the LVR in 1976. Shortly after its arrival, it was loaned to the Blenheim Palace Railway at Woodstock for a short period. (M.Dart)

EAST WHEAL ROSE

111. A panorama of East Wheal Rose includes *Zebedee* on a train waiting to depart to Benny Halt on 27th July 2003. The chimney and engine house of East Wheal Rose mine form a backdrop. (M.Dart)

Other views are included in *Branch Lines to Newquay.*

LAUNCESTON STEAM RAILWAY

The ex-London & South Western Railway route from Halwill to Wadebridge, via Launceston, closed to all traffic on 3rd October 1966. A new railway was laid to the gauge of 600mm, and it started a hundred yards south of the LSWR station at Launceston. It opened on 26th December 1983. The line has been extended in stages, and runs for 2½ miles to New Mills. Locomotive and carriage sheds, workshops, and a motor cycle exhibition are located adjacent to the Launceston terminus in the old gas works area.

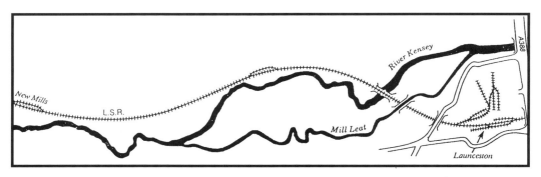

XXXI. This is the diagram of the line in 2003. (Launceston Steam Railway)

Timetable for 2003.

EARLY	Good Friday for 8 days inclusive
SPRING	Bank Holiday Sunday for 6 days
JUNE	Sundays to Wednesdays inclusive
JULY AUGUST and SEPTEMBER	Daily except Saturdays
OCTOBER	Half term week except Saturday

Museum, Café and Shop open from 10.30 a.m.

From Launceston	11.00	11.50	12.45	2.00	2.45	3.35	4.30
From Newmills	11.20	12.10	1.05	2.20	3.05	3.55	4.50

Trains also stop by request at Hunts Crossing for walkers and picnic parties.

MOSELEY INDUSTIAL NARROW GAUGE TRAMWAY & MUSEUM, TOLGUS MOUNT, REDRUTH

120.   This system was originally sited in Cheshire, near Stockport. The owner moved to Cornwall with some of the stock and established a 2ft gauge line at Tumbleydown Farm in late 2001. It is situated at Tolgus Mount, which is about one and a half miles north west of Redruth. At first the line ran for around 400yds, but was extended a further 200yds during late 2003 and early 2004. A train is ready to depart on 4th July 2004 during a visit by Plymouth Railway Circle. Hauling it is 4wD *The Lady D*, which was built by Simplex in 1944. Two 4w battery electric locomotives in the background are appropriately named *Cathode* and *Diode*. (M.Dart)

The standard gauge freight lines of the district are featured in *East Cornwall Mineral Railways* and *West Cornwall Mineral Railways*. Both are by the same author.

MP Middleton Press

EVOLVING THE ULTIMATE RAIL ENCYCLOPEDIA

Easebourne Lane, Midhurst, West Sussex.
GU29 9AZ   Tel:01730 813169

www.middletonpress.co.uk   email:info@middletonpress.co.uk
A-0 906520   B-1 873793   C-1 901706   D-1 904474

OOP Out of Print at time of printing - Please check current availability   **BROCHURE AVAILABLE SHOWING NEW TITLES**